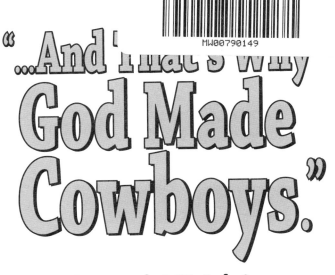

"...And That's Why God Made Cowboys."

A Heapin' Helpin' of Humor & Wisdom

Inspired by Faith

"...And That's Why God Made Cowboys."
ISBN 978-0-9835438-9-3

Published by Product Concept Mfg., Inc.
2175 N. Academy Circle #200, Colorado Springs, CO 80909

©2011 Product Concept Mfg., Inc. All rights reserved.

Sayings not having a credit listed are contributed by writers
for Product Concept Mfg., Inc. or in a rare case,
the author is unknown.

Written and Compiled by N.L. Roloff
in association with Product Concept Mfg., Inc.

"...And That's Why God Made Cowboys."

The LORD bless thee,
and keep thee.

~Numbers 6:24

It's been said that a cowboy is "a man with guts and a horse," but he's so much more than that. In the past, the cowboy helped tame the New Frontier. Today he's a person who lives his life with reverence for God's land and creatures.

A cowboy has a code of honor in his daily dealings, a sense of humor in the way he sees the world, and a sense of duty to friends, family and God. May you enjoy the wisdom, humor and prayers of the cowboy!

Why God
Created Cowboys

God looked upon the sunset
and the prairies brushed with gold
and He knew He had created
a wonder to behold.
He brought soft rains to wash the plains
and make the rivers flow,
and filled the fields with living things,
the deer and buffalo.

He looked upon His work and smiled
for He knew that is was good,
but who'd be the protector of
His mountains, streams and woods?
Who among His creatures was
so honest, true and strong
that he could be entrusted with
this land his whole life long?

God took some earth within His hands
and with it formed a man
of character and courage
to guard His glorious land...
a man tall in the saddle
who would do the best he could.
Yes, God looked upon the cowboy
and He knew His work was good.

~N.L. Roloff

Never approach a bull
from the front,
a horse from the rear,
or a fool from any direction.

Good judgment comes
from experience,
and a lot of that comes
from bad judgment.

~Will Rogers

Cowboys aren't
easy to love,
but they have the
biggest hearts
in the world.

If you can't squat with
your spurs on...
you aint a real cowboy

If you get to thinkin'
you're a person
of some influence,
try orderin' somebody else's
dog around.

~Will Rogers

Sometimes the best
answer is silence.

Shirts that cost more than a
week's worth of groceries
are like horseshoes that cost
more than the horse.

Always drink upstream
from the herd.

~Will Rogers

Use it up,
wear it out,
make do, do without.

Letting the cat out
of the bag is a whole lot
easier than putting
it back in.

~Will Rogers

When you lose,
don't lose the lesson.

When two dogs
fight over a bone,
and a third dog runs
away with it,
one of them dogs
is a lawyer.

Confidence is the
feelin' you have
before you finally
understand the situation.

If your horse doesn't
want to go there,
neither should you.

The biggest troublemaker
you'll probably ever have
to deal with watches you
shave his face in the
mirror every morning.

~Cowboy Proverb

Nobody ever drowned
himself in his own
darn sweat.

A Tombstone
lawyer was pleading
his case to a jury in
Judge Wells Spicer's
court when a burro
beneath the window
started braying loudly.
Lawyer Marcus A.
Smith arose and said,
"If it please the court,
I object to the two
attorneys speaking
at the same time."

Fame is like a shaved pig
with a greased tail,
and it is only after it
has slipped through the
hands of some thousands,
that some fellow,
by mere chance,
holds on to it!

~Davy Crockett

A man doesn't need to
be any higher than on
top of a horse.

The horse is God's gift
to mankind.
~Proverb

I have never been lost,
but I will admit
to being confused for
several weeks.
~Daniel Boone

Nothing does more
for the inside of a man
than the outside of a horse.

When you get to
the end of your rope,
tie a knot and hang on.
~Franklin D. Roosevelt

Making it in life is kind
of like busting broncos.
You're going to get thrown a lot.
The simple secret is
to keep getting back on.

There's two theories to
arguing with a woman.
Neither one works.
~Will Rogers

Sometimes you get
and sometimes you get got.

You can't tell how
good a man or a
watermelon is until they
get thumped.

What the country
needs is dirtier fingernails
and cleaner minds.

~Will Rogers

No philosophers so
thoroughly comprehend
us as dogs and horses.
They see through us
at a glance.

~Herman Melville

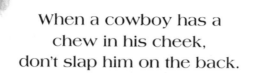

When a cowboy has a
chew in his cheek,
don't slap him on the back.

If you find yourself in
a hole, the first thing to
do is stop digging.

~Will Rogers

Never kick a fresh
cow chip on a hot day.

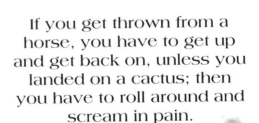

If you get thrown from a
horse, you have to get up
and get back on, unless you
landed on a cactus; then
you have to roll around and
scream in pain.

Don't interfere
with something
that ain't botherin'
you none.

Live a good,
honorable life.
Then when you get
older and think back,
you'll enjoy it all
over again.

When the ranch
is in peace,
no other life
is more perfect.
~Charles Goodnight
(Panhandle Rancher)

After you groom
your horse,
don't forget yourself.

There never was a horse that
couldn't be rode;
Never was a cowboy that
couldn't be throwed.

Broke is what happens
when a cowboy lets his
yearnin's get ahead of
his earnin's.
~Old West Proverb

Boots, chaps
and cowboy hats...
nothin' else matters.

You can tell a true
cowboy by the type of
horse he rides.
~Cowboy Proverb

Never ask a barber if
you need a haircut.
~Old Saying

Any cowboy can
carry a tune.
The trouble comes
when he tries to
unload it.
~Old West Proverb

Conflict follows
wrongdoing
as surely as flies
follow the herd.
~Doc Holiday

Cowboys are stronger
than two red onions.

A horse is worth
more than riches.

~Proverb

When you wallow with
pigs, expect to get dirty.

When a cowboy's too old
to set a bad example,
he hands out good advice.

We should never
reach so high
that we would ever
forget those who
helped us get there.

~Will Rogers

The easiest way to eat crow
is while it's still warm.
The colder it gets,
the harder it is to swaller.

If it don't seem like
it's worth the effort,
it probably ain't.

Generally, you ain't
learnin' nothing
when your mouth's a-jawin'.

If lawyers are disbarred
and clergymen are
defrocked, shouldn't it
follow that cowboys
would be deranged?

After weeks of
beans 'n taters,
even a change to
taters 'n beans is good.

Cowboy Stew...
Throw everything into
the pot but the hair,
horns and holler.
The longer it boils
the better it is.

Let us endeavor so to live
that when we come to die,
even the undertaker
will be sorry.
~Mark Twain

Never let the bull
get between you and
the fence.

As the years go by,
we may not be
as good as we once were,
but we're as good once
as we ever were.

No day is so lousy
it can't be improved
by a nap.

Don't let yesterday use up
too much of today.

~Will Rogers

If you're tryin'
somethin' new,
the fewer people
who know about it
the better.

The best way out
of difficulty
is through it.
~Will Rogers

The trip upstream
may not always
be worth the swim.

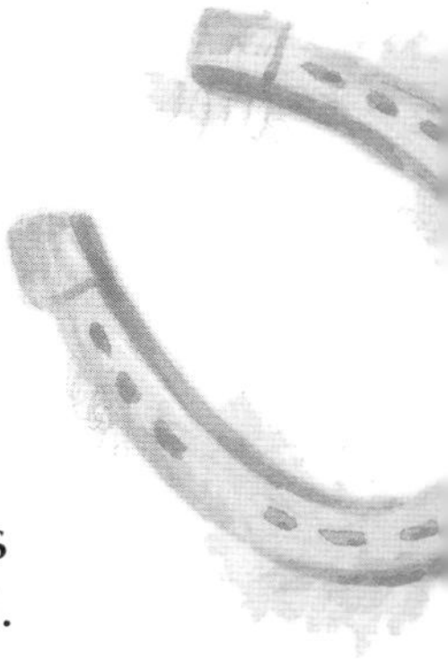

Wearin' gloves and
button-fly jeans means
you better think ahead.

Life isn't so much about
the hand you're dealt
as it is about the way
you play it.

If your horse says no,
you either asked the wrong
question or asked
the question wrong.

The best way
to get a cowboy to do
somethin' is to suggest
he's too old for it.

If you're not makin' dust,
you're eatin' it.

On those days
when you feel like a
movin' target,
just keep movin'!

May your belly never grumble,
may your heart never ache,
may your horse never stumble,
may your cinch never break.
~Cowboy Blessing

Everybody needs a
pot to perk it.

If it's a horse, ride it.
If it's a fence, fix it.
If she's a lady, treat her
like a queen.

You shouldn't touch
another man's woman,
nor should you touch
another man's hat.

...your bucking horses
even painfully real to me,
as I rode one of those
outrages once for nearly
a quarter of a minute.

~Mark Twain
(excerpt from a letter
to Buffalo Bill Cody, 1884)

Never miss
a good chance
to shut up.

~Will Rogers

Don't judge people
by their relatives.

The one that scares ya
the most is the horse
you oughta
jump on first.

It's better to be a has-been
than a never was.

Twenty years down
the road, you'll be a bunch
more disappointed by the
things you didn't do,
than by the things
you did do.

Problems are like broncos,
sometime you just have to
ride 'em out.

To move a mountain,
you have to start
by taking away
the smallest stones.

Yer never too old to teach
or too young to learn.

Forgive your enemies.
It confuses the dickens
out of 'em.

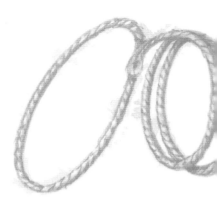

Your buckle don't
shine in the dirt...
get up.

When everyone else
starts gallopin' in
the opposite direction,
a true friend hangs
off a cliff to
throw you a rope.

We're all travelers
in the wilderness of this world,
and the best we can find in our
travels is an honest friend.
~Robert Louis Stevenson

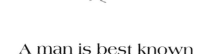

A man is best known
by the company
he avoids.

Do not follow where
the path may lead.
Go instead where there
is no path,
and leave a trail.
~Ralph Waldo Emerson

Horse Sense =
Stable Thinking

Cowboys are like saddles,
the more broke in they are,
the more comfortable
they are to ride with.

If there's a fire
in your belly,
there mighta been
too many beans
in your chili.

Never clean off your boots
where yer thinkin'
of puttin' yer sleepin' bag.

You can
pick yer nose,
and you can pick
yer friends,
but pickin' yer
friend's nose
is just askin'
fer trouble.

Give me a fast horse,
a faithful friend,
a loving woman
and the good Lord
watching over me...
~Amen

A stranger is a friend
I haven't met yet.

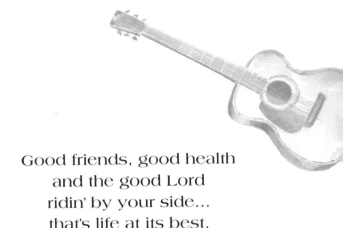

Good friends, good health
and the good Lord
ridin' by your side...
that's life at its best.

Getting up with the sun
and lookin' over
the wide open spaces
that surround us
reminds us of how
great and generous a
friend God is.

A true cowboy
keeps his word,
respects his woman
and stays close to God.

In the wide open
spaces, the golden
prairies and the
mountains high,
we are closer to God
than anywhere
else on earth.

When you get in a tight place
and everything goes against you
till it seems like you can't hold
on another minute, never give
up, for that's just the time and
the place when your strength
will see you through.

Get knocked down
seven times,
get back up eight.

If you want to be
successful,
it's just this simple.
Know what you're
doing. Love what
you're doing.
And believe in what
you're doing.

~Will Rogers

We miss all the
opportunities
we never dare to take.

The best doctor
in the world is a
veterinarian.
He can't ask his
patients what's
the matter. He's just got
to know.
~Will Rogers

The most affectionate
creature in the world is
a wet dog.
~Ambrose Bierce

I was happy in the
midst of dangers
and inconveniences.
~Daniel Boone

Most folks are about as
happy as they make up
their minds to be.
~Abe Lincoln

Cowboys wore "blue jeans"
before it was "cool".

Even the horses know
when somebody is all
hat and no cattle.

Fear less, hope more,
eat less, chew more,
whine less, breathe more,
talk less, say more,
love more and all good things
will come your way.

It's bad luck puttin' on
your left boot first.

Heaven is under our feet,
as well as over our heads.

~Henry David Thoreau

What is life?
It is the flash of a
firefly in the night.
It is the breath of
a buffalo in the
wintertime. It is the
little shadow which
runs across the grass
and loses itself
in the sunset.

~Crowfoot Quote

When you go though life
riskin' nothin'
you risk everything.

Keep away from
people who try to
belittle your ambitions.
Small people always
do that,
but the really great
make you feel
that you, too,
can become great.
~Mark Twain

That cowboy
is richest
whose pleasures
are cheapest.

The worst thing that
can happen to you
may be the best
thing for you,
if you don't let it get
the best of you.

~Will Rogers

Life's truest happiness is found
in the friendships we make
along the way.

Treat people as if
they're what
they ought to be,
and you'll help them
become what they're
capable of being.

~Johann Wolfgang von Goethe

Don't ride behind me,
I may not lead.
Don't ride in front of me,
I may not follow.
Just ride beside me
and be my friend.

Friendship is a
sheltering tree.
~Samuel Taylor Coleridge

Mistakes are part of
the price we pay
for living life to the fullest.

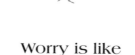

Worry is like
a rockin' horse.
It's something
to do that don't
get you nowhere.

Do what's good for others,
and if people accuse you
of trying to get something out
of it for yourself,
do good anyway.

It's those folks who
desire the good
of their friends for their
friend's own sake
that are the truest
friends.

A cowboy is a man
with guts and a horse.
~William James

Courage is bein' scared
and saddlin' up anyway.

In youth, we learn.
We just don't figger out
what we learned
till we get older!

Keep your fences
horse-high,
pig-tight and
bulls-strong.

Never corner somethin'
meaner than you.

Life is simpler when
you plow around the stump.

Never sell your mule
to buy a plow.

A cowboy never
betrays a trust.

Honesty isn't something
you should flirt with,
you should be married to it.

Speak softly
but mean what you say.

Keep all skunks,
bankers and lawyers
at a distance.

Congress is going
to start tinkering
with the Ten
Commandments
just as soon as they
can find someone in
Washington who
has read them.
~Will Rogers

Just 'cause you
put your boots
in the oven,
that don't make
'em biscuits.

Never give your horse
more attention than
your wife,
unless you like sleepin'
in the barn.

Never name a pig
you're plannin' on eatin'.

Common sense
ain't as common
as you might think.

Do what you have to do
and scratch where you
have to scratch.

Only a fool argues
with a skunk,
a mule or a cook.

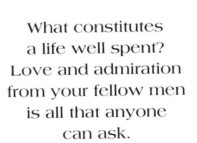

What constitutes
a life well spent?
Love and admiration
from your fellow men
is all that anyone
can ask.

~Will Rogers

You get yourself lost and you're playin' with trouble. No matter whether you're out on a high plain or down in some forest, you got to find your way home. What I do is I scout out a trail broke by any grazing animal...deer or cattle...and follow that trail because it eventually leads to water. Then, when you find a little stream... you follow it down. If you follow water downstream far enough, you'll come to people. 'Course, they may be lost, too. But frankly, all of us lose the trail from time to time, so if you're one of 'em, don't feel too bad.

COWBOY JOE
Take a pound of coffee,
wet it good with water,
boil over a hot fire
for 30 minutes.
Throw a horseshoe in it.
If the shoe sinks,
put in more coffee.

You can't drink coffee
on a runnin' horse.

He'd been ridin'
the range so long,
he knew all the lizards
by their first names.

A cowboy will watch
the sunset because it's
a perfect work of art by
the man upstairs.

My restless,
roaming spirit would
not allow me to remain
at home very long.
~Buffalo Bill

People who fly
into a rage
always make a
bad landing.
~Will Rogers

An old timer is a
man who's had a
lot of interesting
experiences—
some of them true.

Talk slowly,
think quickly.

You must judge a
man's greatness
by how much he
will be missed.

~Will Rogers

Happiness is when
what you think,
what you say
and what you do
are the same thing.

If you don't know
where yer goin',
best not use your spurs.

Don't be spittin'
into the wind.

The best way to
keep your word
is to think twice before
you give it.

When you work
for a man,
ride for his brand,
and treat his cattle as if
they were your own.

A bronc rider should
be light in the head
and heavy in the seat.
~Old West Proverb

Don't ever sell the horse
to buy a saddle.

One good knife
is worth two
of 'most anything else,
'cept women and
horses, of course.
~1885

When you give a
lesson in meanness
to a critter or a person,
don't be surprised if they
learn their lesson.
~Will Rogers

It's hard to put a foot
into a closed mouth.

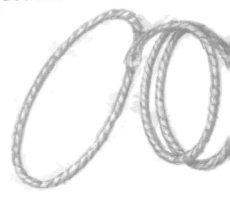

You don't climb out of anything
as quick as you fall in.
~Will Rogers

It don't take a very big person
to carry a grudge.

Don't just grab
the first thing
that comes by.
Know what to
turn down.
~Will Rogers

Scars are Cowboy Tattoos
with better stories.

A bull is like a dancin' partner...
you just have to let him lead.

Some horses
can buck
a man's whiskers
plum off.

No one can make
you wise. You have to
travel your own journey
down life's trail,
make your own mistakes,
and learn from them.
No one else can take
that trip for you.

Don't go milkin' your
neighbor's cow.

Be who you are
and say what you think
and be your own person,
because those who
mind don't matter,
and those who matter
don't mind.

The best sermons
are lived,
not preached.

First try to make
something of yourself,
then try to make the most
of yourself.

Most of the stuff
people worry about
ain't never gonna
happen anyway.

If you're gonna drive
cattle through town,
do it on a Sunday.
There's little traffic
and people
are less disposed
to cuss at ya'.

If somethin' makes
your dog's hackles go up,
it's no time to be
lettin' your guard down.

Live your life
so you're not afraid
to sell your parrot
to the town gossip.

~Will Rogers

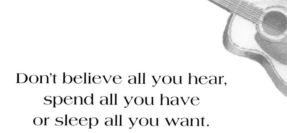

Don't believe all you hear,
spend all you have
or sleep all you want.

God gave us two ears
and one mouth
'cause we learn a whole
lot more from listenin'
than spoutin' off.

Don't judge a man
by the size of his hat
or his horse.
The size of his heart
is what matters.

Always make time
to be alone
with the lady you love,
the horse you ride
and the Lord up above.

Rumor travels faster,
but it don't stay put
as long as truth.

~Will Rogers

It isn't what we don't
know that gets
us in trouble.
It's what we know
that ain't so.

~Will Rogers

May you have the hindsight
to know where you've been,
the foresight to know
where you're goin'
and the insight to know
when you've gone too dang far.

Things ain't what
they used to be...
and they never were.

The time to save is now.
When a dog gets a bone
he doesn't go out and make
a down payment
on a bigger bone.
He buries the one he's got.
~Will Rogers

The higher the horse
you're sittin' on,
the harder the fall.

If it's worth doin',
it's worth doin' right,
so don't hurry none
and do it right
the first time.

When life hands
you lemons,
go find some
city slicker and
trade 'em for a
can o' beans.

You can't put
lipstick on a pig,
but you sure can
send a horse's rear end
to Congress.

When life hands you
a can o' worms,
grab your pole and
go fishin' with 'em.

Never wake a
sleepin' rattler.

Every trail has a
few puddles in it.

When the goin'
gets rough,
and the mountains
get too high
to go over,
God will help us
get around them.

Life is not about
how fast you can run,
or how high you can climb,
but how well you bounce.

When you see
three cowboys ridin' in
a pickup you can tell
which is the smartest...
the one in the middle.
He never drives and
he never has to
git the gate!

Spinnin' a rope is fun
if your neck ain't in it.

No matter what
you weigh,
the little fellow is
your equal on a horse.

~Will Rogers

When you ask
for free advice,
you get exactly
what you paid for.

Always be sure
you're in the right,
then get on with it.

It's not how many
times you get
bucked off that counts.
It's how many
times you saddle back up
that matters.

Never take down
another man's fence.

Don't go in if you
don't know the way out.

Never drive black cattle
in the dark.

A man, a horse
and a dog
never get weary of
each other's company.

No creature on earth
is more noble, more
patient, more obedient,
and more plain ol' helpful
than a good horse, well
broke by the man who
loves her dear. On a hot
day in the middle of
no-place, she's also the
best lookin' gal anywhere,
and if they made a bride's
gown to fit a Paint Horse,
I'd soon marry the horse
as a woman but I don't
know of a horse who'd
have me.

~Oliver Curtis, 1912

God first made Man.
He thought better of it
and made Woman.
When He got time He made
the Horse, which has the
courage and spirit
of the Man and the beauty and
grace of the Woman.

~Brazilian Saying

Even if a ranch hand
intends to loaf,
he gets up in time
to get an early start.

When in doubt,
let your horse
do the thinkin'.

If you haven't fallen
off a horse...
then you haven't been
ridin' long enough.

Never miss a chance
to rest your horse.

There is no secret
so close as that
between a rider
and his horse.
~R.S. Surtees

Tell a gelding,
ask a stallion,
discuss it with a mare.

He knows when
you're happy,
He knows when
you're comfortable,
He knows when
you're confident,
And he *always* knows
when you have carrots.

No matter where
you ride to,
that's where you are.

When you don't know
if you're comin' or goin',
let your horse decide.

The hardest thing
about learnin' to ride a horse
is the ground.

If you want a stable
friendship, get a horse.

No hour is lost spent
in the saddle.

Horse sense is the
thing a horse has
that keeps it from
betting on people.
~W.C. Fields

Animals are such
agreeable friends—
they ask no questions,
they pass no criticisms.
~George Eliot

To ride a horse
is to ride the sky.

When God created the
horse, He spoke to the
magnificent creature:
I have made thee
without equal. All the
treasures of the earth lie
between your eyes...
Thou shalt fly
without wings.

The spirit of the wild
horse is the same after
years of riding as it was
before he ever felt a
rope, and there's no
human in the world wants
to preserve that spirit in
the horse like a cowboy
does; he's the one what
knows better than
anybody else that a horse
with a broken spirit is not
a horse at all.

~William James

God forbid that I
should go to a heaven
in which there
are no horses.

~R. B. Cunnighame-Graham
(letter to Theodore Roosevelt, 1917)

There are three things a
cowboy never forgets:
his first girl, his mom's
home-cookin' and a
great horse.

As a good horse is not
very apt to jump over
a bank, if left to
guide himself,
I let mine pick
his own way.

~Buffalo Bill

Ridin' is the art
of keepin the
horse between you
and the ground.

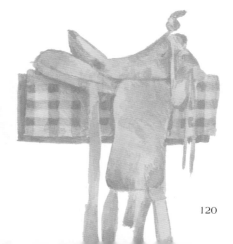

I spent most of my
life ridin' horses.
The rest of it
I just wasted.

A good horse
makes the miles shorter.

When you're feelin'
down, saddle up.

Spending many hours
in the saddle gives a guy
lots of time to think.
That's why so many
cowboys turn out
to be philosphers.

A dog may be
man's best friend,
but the horse
wrote history.

Nearly all I know I have learned from a cow.... You'd be surprised just how much you can learn from a cow....Cows are regular in their habits, they go to the same place in the range to graze, they want to drink from the same place in the water trough, they are the best civil engineers you can find, and they can pick out the best possible grade to climb a mountain. A cow trail is always the best way to get out of a deep canyon. Follow a cow trail and you will come to water, or you will find the way out of a rough country if you are lost.

~Drew Rush, 1882

Only cows know
why they stampede,
and they ain't talkin'.

Talkin' about music...
I used to own
a saxophone,
but traded it off for
a cow. Made about the
same noise and gave
milk besides.

~Anonymous Cowboy

They shore ain't pretty
and they don't smell good,
but there's somethin' about a
cow that makes the man
that owns her feel like he's
got money in his purse.

~Spin Lucette, 1869

The only way
to drive cattle fast
is slowly.

While it is easy to
brand a calf, one has to
keep a sharp lookout
on its mother. As soon as
she hears the cry of
her young, she will come
at you like an express torrent.

If you teach a
calf to lead,
the old cow
will follow.

Don't ever get between
a calf and its mother.

A man who can't
sing to calm a nervous
cow ain't enough cowboy
to hold the job. At night,
cows get nervous,
and anything can make 'em
jump up and start,
so you gotta have
a man with a voice
good enough to
keep 'em quiet.
~1916

The
Bull Rider's
Prayer

As I live the Cowboy Way,
Protection is what I pray,
I don't know my Fate,
Outside of the gate.
If my ride sees trouble,
Send Angels on the double,
For in You the Lord I rest,
Let my life pass Your test.
By pure grace I am saved,
Lord, ride with me,
That's the Cowboy Way,
And what bull riders pray.

~Amen

Cowboy's
Rodeo Prayer

Our gracious and Heavenly
Father, we pause in the midst of
this festive occasion,
mindful and thoughtful of the
guidance that You have given
us. We would ask, today Lord,
that You be with us in this rodeo
arena as we pray You will also
be with us in life's arena.

As cowboys, Lord, we don't
ask for any special favors in the
arena today. We only ask that
You will let us compete
in this event, and in life, as you
did for us. We don't ask that we
never break a barrier,
draw a steer that won't lay,
draw around a chute fighting
horse, or a bull that is
impossible to ride.

Help us to compete in life
as honest as the horse we ride;
in a manner as clean and pure
as the wind that blows across
this great land;
so when we make that last ride,
that we know is inevitable
to the country up there where
the grass is green and lush
and stirrup high and the water
runs clean and clear;
You will tell us, as our last judge,
that our entry fees are paid.
We ask these things
in Christ's name.

~Amen

End
of the Trail

When life is over and my race is run,
when death shadows gather
and my time has come,
When I've rode my last horse
and have turned my last steer,
When my soul has winged its way
to that last frontier,
When my grave's been dug
and I've been laid to rest,
Please let it be in the far, far West.

~Amen

God
of the Open

God of the open, though I am so simple
Out in the wind I can travel with you,
Noons when the hot mesas ripple and dimple,
Nights when the stars glitter cool in the blue.
Too far you stand for the reach of my hand,
Yet I can feel your big heart as it beats
Friendly and warm in the sun or the storm.
Are you the same as the God of the streets?

Yours is the sunny blue roof I ride under;
Mountain and plain are the house you have made.
Sometimes it roars with the wind and the thunder
But in your house I am never afraid.
He? Oh they give him the license to live,
Aim in their ledgers, to pay him his due,
Gather by herds to present him with words—
Words! What are words when my heart talks with you?

God of the open,
forgive an old ranger
Penned among walls where
he never sees through.
Well do I know, though their God
seems a stranger,
Earth has no room
for another like you.
Shut out the roll of the
wheels from my soul;
Send me a wind that
is singing and sweet
Into this place where
the smoke dims your face.
Help me see you in
the God of the street.
~Badger Clark

Prayer

When they lay me
down to rest
Put my spurs and rope
upon my chest.
Get my friends
to carry me
and then go turn
my horses free.

Blessing

May those who love us, love us;
and those who don't love us,
may God turn their hearts;
and if He doesn't turn their hearts,
may He turn their ankles
so we'll know 'em by their limpin'.

Blessing

May the trail rise up to meet you,
may the wind be ever at your back,
may the sun shine warm
upon your face
and the rain fall softly
on your fields and herd,
and until we meet again,
may God hold you
in the hollow of His hand.

Blessing

May God always give you
a campfire to warm you,
a good woman to charm you,
His sheltering love so that
nothing can harm you;
Good friends to cheer you,
your faithful horse near you,
and whenever you pray,
Heaven to hear you.

A Cowboy's Prayer

by Badger Clark
(Written for Mother in 1906)

Oh Lord, I've never lived where churches grow.

I love creation better as it stood

That day You finished it so long ago

And looked upon Your work and called it good.

I know that others find You in the light

That's sifted down through tinted window panes,

And yet I seem to feel You near tonight

In this dim, quiet starlight on the plains.

I thank You, Lord, that I am placed so well,

That You have made my freedom so complete;

That I'm no slave of whistle, clock or bell,

Nor weak-eyed prisoner of wall and street.

Just let me live my life as I've begun

And give me work that's open to the sky;

Make me a pardner of the wind and sun,

And I won't ask a life that's soft or high.

Let me be easy on the man that's down;
Let me be square and generous with all.
I'm careless sometimes, Lord, when I'm in town,
But never let 'em say I'm mean or small!
Make me as big and open as the plains,
As honest as the hawse between my knees,
Clean as the wind that blows behind the rains,
Free as the hawk that circles down the breeze!